Vital Signs

Jesus's Dying Words
Bring Hope

 *Book 1*

Forgiveness
and Paradise

The Power of
Relentless Grace

Author Website: www.batesbooks.co.uk
fb.me/batesbooks

TIMELESS
PUBLICATIONS LTD

Timeless Publications Ltd
Belvedere Park
Castlerock
Northern Ireland

Printed in the United Kingdom
First Printing 2017

ISBN 978-0-9957886-3-3

Timeless Publications Ltd
www.timelesspublications.co.uk

All photographs not cited are used courtesy of www.pixabay.com.

Dedication

To all those who have been struggling with life and have found strength in the risen Lord.

Contents

Acknowledgements

I would like to give thanks to my editor, Renee De Assis, for her professionalism, encouragement, research input, and devotion to Christ shown throughout this project. Also the very professional services of Erin Brown, who carried out the necessary proofreading of the text.

How to Use
This Book

This book can be used in a variety of ways. It can be read for personal devotion by simply navigating past the sections marked for small group Bible study. It can be studied in four separate sessions or as one session. In order to study it as one session, simply read the book and then explore the questions found in Session Four of this booklet. Session Four is the longest of all sessions in order to facilitate one stand-alone small group Bible study.

Some useful small group Bible study resources can be located on our website, www.batesbooks.co.uk. These resources are free for those who purchase this booklet and resources include a PowerPoint presentation and other helpful materials. Navigate to the website, click on the Vital Signs, and use the following password: VS98745673BB.

Introduction to *Vital Signs*

Setting the Scene

I often write in cafés, believing coffee to be the perfect stimulant to creative writing. On this particular morning, I stare out the window, fingers welded motionless to the keyboard. A leaf flutters in the wind as it is caressed by the gentle breeze, and for a brief moment, sunshine floods every corner of the courtyard.

Though distant, I hear the noise of children playing and a dog barking. Closer, the clinking of spoons as a mother feeds her baby and the waitress clearing away dishes create the white noise of daily life, which is strangely comforting, or at least it would be if today were normal . . . but it isn't, as my mind drifts to an earlier event.

The chamber of noise returns as I drift back to the present. The mother is still feeding her baby, the dog is still barking, and the couple at the next table have not averted their gazes from today's headlines. Their lives are no doubt also comforted by familiar sounds and daily routines. But for one lady, life will never be the same again. And I, too, am struggling to reconcile the beauty of today's sunshine with the harsh reality of human existence.

A few days previous I had received a phone call on my mobile. It was the emergency department of a nearby hospital. A serious accident had involved one of my church elders. The nurse found it difficult to retain her professional composer, for she knew Michael, and the tremble in her voice indicated her deepest concerns.

Whilst travelling I listen to the radio—but not that day. Instead, I was subdued and apprehensive; the journey to the hospital seemed to last forever. The nurse met me at the door and her body language failed to hide her distress. Fearful of what I would encounter, I braced myself. As I walked through the double doors to Michael's room, I swiveled to my left, and before I had the opportunity to access his injuries, I caught Sally's eyes. Tearfully we embraced. The only sound was the rhythm of the ventilator assisting her husband's breathing.

It had been a tragic accident. Sally and Michael's day had begun with an ever-increasing excitement. This desperately in love couple had been planning a special holiday. The next morning they were to have travelled thousands of miles away to celebrate their fortieth wedding anniversary. Sally had decided to complete a few tasks not far from home; Michael, on the other hand, had planned not to waste time in her absence but attend to some outstanding jobs. Due to inclement weather conditions, he had aborted an earlier attempt to clean the gutters, but this day presented a perfect opportunity. Removing leaves from the spouting was a simple job, requiring only minutes to rectify.

A neighbour frequently walked his dog past the couple's house and often nodded as Michael popped up from behind a shrub to greet him with his usual infectious smile. Not seeing Michael on this morning, he continued just a hundred yards to the nearby church and then turned around, returning the way he had come. It was then he noticed Michael, motionless on the ground, the ladder lying beside him. The neighbour had quickly dialed 999. In a matter of minutes the ambulance had arrived.

As Sally and I released our embrace, I looked at Michael lying motionless on the bed. I felt powerless. What can you say in the face of tragedy? The more you love someone, the greater the heartache when you are forced to let go. I knew that for Sally the next few days were going to be a tough challenge.

It soon became clear that Michael would not recover. The following day we met with the consultant. He tried his best to finely balance his emotions and professional training. I did not envy his task of pronouncing Michael dead while seeking to offer comfort to the grieving. He did so with admirable compassion, no doubt experienced in its delivery. However, Sally, with resolute composure, raised her head and said, "It was his time to go."

Her words lingered, as if taking on a life of their own. Each word pounding with a separate heartbeat. Each word hanging in mid-air as they surveyed the landscape of broken hearts. God has promised that his words would not return to him void, but the question was, on whose heart would they land? Would it be the consultant's? Perhaps not, for he may have heard them before, and a life of pain may have sufficiently inoculated him against their desired intent. Would they find a welcome home with the family? Possibly, but, then again, my experience had taught me that such a phrase rarely finds a warm home in the hearts of those frozen with grief.

But those words would not disappear. As they searched the room's occupants, they fixed their attention on me. Locked in an unfriendly gaze, our eyes met. I wondered how on earth it had been Michael's time to go. It was only last year I had installed him as an elder in our church. He had taken early retirement to enjoy his health, home, wife, family, and church. He was a devoted Christian who had transferred his faith into his business practices. Admired by his customers, loved by the community, and respected by the church, Michael had served God with passion, selflessness, and infectious enthusiasm. I could easily think of others who had run their course, but surely Michael had many laps of the track still to compete. The race half run and the fight only half over, how could time have been called on his life? And how could Sally have said with such reassurance that it was his time to go? Her words had stood knocking at the door of my heart for a few days before I would eventually invite them in.

The clatter of cutlery, children crying, and the old couple still not speaking pull me back into the real world of my favourite café. My enjoyment of the bright sunshine outside is tempered by the sad reality of life's most difficult moments. Today I am only too aware that for every person walking through the courtyard, stacking trays, cleaning a child's nose, or adjusting their glasses to read the fine print of a newspaper, life is a mix of both blessing and pain, laughter and tears.

Michael's death was difficult, and Sally's words, "It was his time to go," initially compounded it. Clearly a bittersweet moment. Pain and blessing contained in the same cup. We were being asked to consume both, as if they had the same nutritional value. And maybe that is the apparent contradiction we have to live with. That in death we find life, and that hope's most fertile soil is despair. Jesus had stopped the battle—mid-fight—raised Michael's arm, and announced him the true winner.

For a few days we lived in the presence of machines, every green line, flashing red light, beep, blip, and tone recording Michael's vital signs. But how do we read them? Surrounded by wires, tubes, and flashing lights, we would have wept without hope. It is true that Sally and I did weep, but we can honestly say we did not grieve as those without hope, but with a sure and certain resurrection to eternal life. But why? In the face of such apparent tragedy, why such hope, why such optimism? What gave us the confidence to stand defiant in the face of death? When the serpent bites and the poisonous venom of death pulsates through our veins, how is the sting and victory of death removed?

One thing is certain: Our defiant stance in the face of death did not emerge from humanly engineered strength, fortitude, or blissful stupidity. Its foundation did not appear under western skies and lily-white clouds. The reason for our hope is grounded on Calvary's hill.

Under the dark skies of Jerusalem, a drama had unfolded, a drama of cosmic proportions. With the light fading, three silhouetted crosses marked the skyline. A diverse audience gathered. Their attendance shaped by diverse reasons. The soldiers, obliged by duty, fondled the dice, hoping that the gods would show favour. A robe of royal colour their prize for good fortune. Two thieves, compelled under sentence, watched the ensuing drama. With reserved seats, these two were Jesus's captive audience.

Religious leaders volunteered to scrutinise Jesus's execution, making sure that this religious irritant and blasphemer was finally eliminated. Others mingled, not sure why they found themselves at the foot of the cross. Perhaps they attended out of curiosity, entertainment, disbelief, or sheer boredom. Whatever had brought them together would not hold them for long. In a matter of hours, the crowd would disperse, and with tomorrow's sunrise, they would resume life as usual. Well, perhaps most would. Huddled underneath an imposing skyline, a few watchers clung to each other. They had once held Jesus in the same way, but now he was out of reach.

The dark clouds increased as Jesus's heartbeat diminished. A life once vibrant now pulsated with agonising pain. His words that had echoed across the Mount of Olives could barely be heard above the capricious crowd. With every slowing heartbeat, his vital signs dropped as if in sync with his disciples' drooping heads.

But what if this moment was planned? What if Sally was right, that it was Jesus's time to go? Had Jesus not said as much when he issued those immortal words, "My time has come"? And if this is true, then what appeared to be a cosmic tragedy was ironically his greatest triumph. Impaled upon a cross, his backstory, not yet fully understood, was emerging center stage.

In full view of those gathered, his vital signs were failing, but shortly after his heart would stop, and start again, the pounding of hearts would begin. In perhaps one of the strangest passages in the Bible we read, "And the tombs broke open. The bodies of many holy people who had died were raised to life. They came out of the tombs after Jesus' resurrection and went into the holy city and appeared to many people" (Matthew 27:52–53). His vital signs would stop so that ours could truly begin. Those who walked in Jerusalem that day saw the fulfillment of God's promise that the seed of the woman would truly bruise the head of the serpent. Death's icy fingers clutched at the heart of Jesus, but they dissolved like snow in the heat of his love. Those who walked the streets of Jerusalem that day, when Jesus breathed his last, would soon be walking the streets of heaven; and the moment Michael breathed his last, so would he.

What gave Sally hope? It is the very thing that gives every believer hope. That, as God's Son, Jesus could promise something no one else could. "I go to prepare and place for you ... and if I go and prepare a place for you I will come again and take you to be where I am" (John 14:2–3 NRSV). Jesus's vital signs had to stop that day so that our hearts could pound with a strength and fullness never before experienced. He did truly come to give us life, and life to the full.

In this book series, you will discover that what appeared to be a dark, miserable, godforsaken day over Jerusalem was the most glorious of all time. During the agony of the cross, where fear, despair, and heart-pounding sadness filled the air, Jesus's dying words brought hope.

Book 1

Forgiveness and Paradise

The Power of
Relentless Grace

Death Casts Its Shadow

I STAND at many gravesides. Irish burials are a densely populated occasion. With sullen expressions, we bunch together under grey skies. An umbrella may defend us against the rain, but little can defend us against a broken heart. We have little power over the elements and even less power over death. Like an unwelcomed intruder, death bypasses our defenses and takes what is precious. It comes as a thief in the night and suffocates the breath from our loved ones. The icy wind of death leaves our hearts frozen in time. We can no longer imagine a life with our beloved, and we do not want to imagine a life without them.

Death changes everything. Our past is remembered differently. The deceased seem to appear in every photograph, and our memories have them present at every significant event. They become saints in a land of sinners. We paint them in colour against a world etched in grey.

As a pastor I know the heartache of loss. I have buried infant children, teenage sons and daughters, and dearly loved parents. I have cried tears of lament and wept at the

> "To stand here is also to stand in the center of so much that is wounded and wrong in this nation and world, in a well of catastrophe that is, at the same time, a center which springs amazing grace."
> HEIDI NEUMARK,
> *Breathing Space*

11

world's brokenness. My greatest challenge is not a lack of identity with grief, for I, too, have lost family and friends. My greatest challenge is how to effectively articulate what the dead meant to those they leave behind, no matter how brief a tribute. I will ponder, pray, and repeatedly redraft each narrative so that nothing of importance is missed. The pastoral gift to those who are grieving is to be succinct but not dispassionately brief. We do not want to linger at death, but we do want to pause and remember the beauty of a life well lived. We offer memories to one another that warm frozen hearts, and, as a pastor, I do my best to provide images that comfort and heal.

As the few remaining disciples of Jesus stand beneath the cross, the bitter chill of death permeates the air. At first glance, each gospel writer appears incapable of breathing warmth into Calvary's frozen landscape. As if the pain of remembering Jesus's death means that succinctness gives way to dispassionate brevity. Two criminals, three impending deaths at a place called *the skull*. The scandalous event is matched with indifference among soldiers who gamble over a dying man's garments. The gospel artist draws this scene in charcoal grey because no palette of colours can be found. Yet we are invited to linger at the cross and look beyond the pain of our grief to see in the portrait one man of *colour* set against the backdrop of greys.

If you are using this as a four-part Bible study, please refer to Session One on pages 43–47

Words of Healing

SPEECHLESS, the disciples huddle at the cross. What words can articulate their grief? They find no words to comfort one another, let alone words to comfort a dying friend. As Jesus gasps for breath, a knife pierces their souls, every momentary discomfort a new blade entering their hearts. Paralysed by what they could not fix, they stand motionless and speechless.

Many of us have experienced that silence in our lives. Faced with the injustice and tragedy of death, we have nothing to say. As a pastor, I have learned that silence, at times, can be my only response.

When she was thirteen years old, Janice lost her mother. Her brother died a short two years later. I first met her after hearing about her husband's death. He was only forty years old when killed in a tragic car accident. As we paid tribute to him at the funeral, I was conscious of her agonising loss. She was not a church attender but had welcomed me into her home on several occasions. Surrounded by her three children, the family grieved their loss, Janice's childhood bereavement aggravated her present grief.

A few years later, Janice's son went missing. The young lad was only seventeen and had been out with friends. He had gone for a walk on his own but had not returned home. His mother became anxious when she realised he was missing. The community was alerted. I called to offer comfort and reassured Janice, "He probably

spent the night with friends, oblivious to your worry." Although Janice informed the police, they told her he had not been missing long enough for the national public to be alerted.

Residents of the housing community searched night and day, until he was officially recognised as a missing person. It was then Janice asked me to speak on national television on behalf of the family.

Janice and I sat together in the interview room while the press officer briefed me on how to address the television crew. Nervous at the prospect of staring down a camera lens, my heart fluttered. As I took a deep breath to slow my heart rate, the door opened. A man in uniform signaled to the female police officer to exit the room. They returned a few minutes later. When I saw their expressions, my heart sank.

"A spotter helicopter has noticed a body in the water. We can't identity if it is a teenager or adult, but we have sent our ground team in to take a look," the female officer softly explained. "I will leave you with your pastor until we can investigate a little further."

The door gently closed behind me. It was the longest silence I have ever experienced. I had no words to comfort the grieving and frightened mother, nothing to say. Silently we embraced. Glancing at each other, the windows of our souls revealed unspoken heartache. I have learned over the years that sometimes it is better just to feel empty rather than utter the hollow ring of mistimed words. In our grief we simply walked together, realising the toughness of the terrain.

When Job was ill, his comforters spoke too much. At the cross, Jesus's disciples had little to say. Why does silence feel awkward? Jesus's opponents had much to say at the foot of the cross, but not so his disciples. Their hearts bled just like Jesus's wounds, their vocabulary locked up in their sadness. When confronted with grief, offering fewer words might provide much more comfort. Pious pretensions rarely ease our pain. However, Jesus's short phrases revealed healing of cosmic proportions.

"I have heard many things like these; you are miserable comforters, all of you! Will your long-winded speeches never end? What ails you that you keep arguing?
Job 16:2–13

Perhaps confronted with the world's brokenness, we need to say less, not more.

Sadness may have hit your home, or tragedy engulfed a friend. The thought of what to say has kept you awake for hours, watching each second pass until the dawn breaks. You have rehearsed what you would like to say, but it has a hollow ring. Perhaps you need to join the grieving at the foot of the cross. Stand with them in silence. Your presence may be all that is truly required.

"There are times when God asks nothing of his children except silence, patience and tears."
CHARLES SEYMOUR ROBINSON, 19th century Presbyterian Pastor

Two Thieves

IF ONLY the two thieves had followed the disciples' silence. When we collate the gospel record, we find that both thieves, at least for a time, said too much and with harsh insensitivity. Like the soldiers and the crowd, they refused to let a dying man die in peace. "He saved others; let him save himself if he is the Christ of God, the Chosen One." The soldiers also mocked him. They offered him wine vinegar and said, "If you are the king of the Jews, save yourself" (Luke 23:35–37).

Eventually, one of the criminals detected a cruel note in the choral of criticism against Jesus. For a brief time, he fell silent like the disciples. Eventually he broke the silence, "'Don't you fear God,' he said, 'since you are under the same sentence? We are punished justly, for we are getting what our deeds deserve. But this man has done nothing wrong'" (vv. 40–41).

The repentant criminal said, "'Jesus, remember me when you come into your kingdom.' Jesus answered him, 'Truly I tell you, today you will be with me in paradise'" (vv. 42–43)

If you are using this as a four-part Bible study, please refer to Session Two on pages 49–54

Relentless Grace

HOW WOULD our priorities change if we knew we had very few hours to live? We may prioritise our lives, sharpen our reflections, and choose our words more carefully. The recognition of our own mortality focuses our thoughts. We reflect upon the direction of our lives, the relationships we have nurtured—perhaps even those we need to amend. The endless flow of chatter is stilted by the heart-wrenching knowledge of our impending departure. Take heart, for it is not the time we have left that matters but what we say and do with what remains.

Though metal spikes impaled Jesus's body upon dead wood, his words would carry life to future generations. As his dying breath could be counted in minutes, not days, there remained limited time for his final words. He had only moments to demonstrate the extent of his grace and offer his final peace. Jesus hung by nails for three hours in excruciating pain, hearing the cries and malicious taunts of the mocking crowd.

Two thieves who had chosen to live an irresponsible life hung on either side of him and were paying the price for their crimes.

Amid the cries for punishment and venom spewed from the crowd, a drama of relentless grace was unfolding. An innocent man hung on a tree, surrounded by a forest of profanity. He who "knew no sin" (2 Corinthians 5:21) was being "numbered amongst the transgressors" (Luke 22:37 NRSV).

For a time both thieves hurled insults at Jesus, but grace absorbed their charges. Sin is hard to suppress, even in death. The unrepentant criminal found it within him, in spite of his circumstances, to mock Jesus. A man facing his own mortality summoned enough oxygen to belittle Jesus in his last few words.

Under the bleak skies of Jerusalem, the first criminal disregarded Jesus's offer. Jesus showed tremendous grace and courage, yet the unrepentant criminal remained unconvinced. The identity of the criminal and the nature of his theft are unknown. His victims remain anonymous. Yet his words are immortalized as sin's defiance against grace; a refusal to embrace compassion amid death, pain, humiliation, and punishment. We can only speculate as to why he felt it necessary to resist grace. He may have experienced very little grace

"The point we desperately need to grasp is that forgiveness is not the same thing as tolerance. We are told again and again today that we must be 'inclusive'; that Jesus welcomed all kinds of people just as they were; that the church believes in forgiveness and therefore we should remarry divorcees without question, reinstate employees who were sacked for dishonesty, allow convicted pedophiles back into children's work—actually, we don't normally say the last of these, which shows that we have retained at least some vestiges of common sense. But forgiveness is not the same as tolerance. It is not the same as inclusivity. It is not the same as indifference, whether personal or moral. Forgiveness doesn't mean that we don't take evil seriously after all; it means that we do."

N.T. WRIGHT,
Evil and the Justice of God

in his life. The world may have been harsh to him. He may not have had his family with him at the cross. The kind words of Jesus towards his own mother and family, who stood at the foot of the cross, may have served as a painful reminder of a world the thief did not recognise or possess. He was guilty of stealing objects, but the ultimate thief had stolen his life. The sadness of his state and the world he represents I find hard to articulate, even in writing. Yet he may have nursed his wounds that day and ignored the very person "wounded" for his transgressions.

In the midst of this hideous spectacle, Jesus extended grace and hope to us all. With relentless mercy towards the undeserving, Jesus absorbed their insults. Consistent with his sinless life, he did not return evil for evil, even though he was contemplating his own death.

> "Mercy forgave the thief on the cross, grace escorted him to paradise."
>
> MAX LUCADO, *Grace: More Than We Deserve, Greater Than We Imagine*

The gospel narrative is full of surprise. Always under scrutiny, Jesus kept questionable company. Earthly parents may have disapproved of such undesirables, but such company pleased his heavenly Father. Jesus made friends with the most unlikely characters. Tax collectors and sinners were his dinner companions; a Samaritan was refreshed by Jesus's living waters; lepers were healed; the faith of Gentiles was praised; a prostitute was permitted to pour oil over his feet; an adulterous woman was forgiven; and now he hung on tree between two criminals. In death, as in life, he was "numbered among the transgressors." All of them had one thing in common: the recognition of their need and an awareness of Christ's uniqueness. Yet he always extended hope to those who willingly received it.

These two thieves may have deprived others of their possessions, but no amount of theft would alleviate their poverty of spirit. Jesus's mission had always been to seek and save the lost. From the very beginning he had declared his intent:

> The Spirit of the Lord is on me,
> because he has anointed me
> to proclaim good news to the poor.
> He has sent me to proclaim freedom for the prisoners
> and recovery of sight for the blind,
> to set the oppressed free,
> to proclaim the year of the Lord's favour.
> (Luke 4:18–19)

*"We cannot grasp the significance of Jesus Christ apart from his relationships with the persons—both divine and human—who enter his life, **from** whom he receives his life and **for** whom he gives his life."*
JOHN NAVONE, S.J.,
Seeking God in Story

A thief, not a theologian, hung on the cross next to Jesus, yet what was revealed to him is often concealed from the worldly wise:

1. Man must fear God
2. The thief was getting the just punishment for his crimes
3. Jesus was an innocent man
4. Jesus was a heavenly ruler

In that moment, the thief became aware of his sin and moved towards God, believing that repentance and forgiveness may still be possible. His mind tortured with regret, the thief needed to find relief. The agony of heart caused by his offences was as painful as the spikes that crushed his bones. The laws of the land he had ignored now mocked him as he was pinned against that tree. The broken body a painful reminder of a broken life. Did anyone else care for this impaled perpetrator of crime? Or was Jesus the only one filled with compassion? Were his victims within earshot as he asked for mercy? Did they smile as they watched him grimace in pain? He had deprived them of their property, now he must forfeit his life in what appeared to many an appropriate exchange.

Against the stench of impending death, the aroma of divine grace filled the air. With depleted lungs, Jesus tenderly responded to the penitent thief, "Today you will be with me in paradise" (Luke 23:43). The tragedy of a wasted lifetime reversed in a pivotal moment! Like the parable of the workers coming into the kingdom, they all received the same reward no matter how long they had been working (Matthew 20:1–16). While we may be rewarded in heaven, heaven is not our reward. It always was and must remain a gift of Jesus's love, atonement, and astonishing grace. In response to the repentant thief, Jesus embraced, accepted, and welcomed him into the kingdom of heaven.

Jesus's physical pain and exhaustion was extreme. Whilst his life ebbed away, his grace lingered, its fragrance dispelling the stench of death. In an ever-changing world, his consistent grace becomes our greatest comfort.

Isn't that wonderful? This story is saturated with grace, and it reveals the possibilities of pivotal moments and life-changing encounters. Three men were facing their last moments: one was the perfect sacrifice, one was a repentant sinner, and one was unrepentant. Jesus extended the gift of grace to all who were in earshot of the cross, and still does even to this day.

*"I'm not going to Heaven because I have preached to great crowds or read the Bible many times. I'm going to Heaven just like the **thief on the cross** who said in that last moment: 'Lord, remember me."*
BILLY GRAHAM,
American Evangelist

A Life-Changing Moment

Christianity is not about religion. It's about faith, about being held, about being forgiven. It's about finding joy and finding home.

BEAR GRYLLS

THE REPENTANT THIEF found faith, forgiveness, and an eternal home. This life-changing moment was priceless. The revelation of Jesus's innocence and the thief's daunting recognition of his own unworthiness could have been a catalyst for despair. What if Jesus had rejected this thief's cry for help and consideration? We need not contemplate this question because grace prevailed and a sinner found a new home. In just a few moments Jesus would die, and, ironically, during death this thief experienced eternal life. Though a thief welded to a tree by spikes, he found liberation in his dying breath. As he exhaled his last, he inhaled his next breath in paradise. A day that began with an earthly death sentence ended with a heavenly pardon. The thief died for his crimes, but he was not condemned to an eternity away from God. He received a pardon that no earthly authority could issue. A day that started with tragedy ended in triumph for one thief. An encounter with Jesus became pivotal in the life of this wretched man.

Such encounters still happen. It is what gives hope to those who feel alienated by their sins. There is a way towards God for all who have erred. This is our abiding hope. The prodigal has an advocate in Christ. You may be inches from death and still hear those life-changing words, "Today you will be with me in paradise." No matter how bleak your world, grace can dispel its darkness.

"These texts bear witness to the power of God for new life. That is why we are here. God is at work giving new life."
WALTER BRUGGEMANN,
The Collected Sermons of Walter Bruggemann

If you are using this as a four-part Bible study, please refer to Session Three on pages 55–59

Two Different Responses

HERE WE SEE two very different responses to the same life circumstances. Jesus offered the same forgiveness and grace, without discrimination. His love for both thieves was the same. He extended his love to both, but only one embraced Jesus. They were still breathing, even though they were breathing their last. Eternity was *minutes* away, but an opportunity still remained.

It is never too late for you to experience the God of relentless grace. No matter how many years you have wasted. No matter how many moments you have refused God's advances. As a pastor, I have stood at the bedsides of many dying people and asked myself, "Have they made their peace with God? Are they ready to be received into heaven? Have they been saved by God's grace?"

God's grace may not be something you think about every day, but as a pastor I think about it often. How wonderful it is to stand at the bedside of those who are willing to receive Christ. When suddenly they recognise that they have need of him. When they grip your hand with an assurance that they will soon meet Jesus.

I remember sitting beside the bed of a dying missionary wasted by cancer. She lay motionless as we prayed together before she was ushered into heaven. I whispered in her ear, "We will dance in heaven one day soon." The pleasure of heaven is a paradise beyond description, and this missionary had no regrets. She would soon see her Saviour.

In that moment of death, thoughts of a heavenly home flood the hearts of those who are dying. Our bodies may decay but not our hope. In final moments, a promise will soon be realised. Jesus said, "And if I go and prepare a place for you, I will come again and take you to be with me that you also may be where I am" (John 14:3).

The grey skies of Jerusalem receded for a thief and exploded into full color, as it will for each one of us. Yet the sadness still remains. One cross lingers as a lonely reminder of humanity's defiance against the backdrop of grace.

We Are Not All the Same

THIS STORY reminds us that we are not all the same. The hardened criminal is still hard of heart, defiant to the last, even with death approaching and the light fading. As his vital signs begin to drop, his heart remained hard.

How many young people believe that their earthly lives carry on forever? That they will adjust their spiritual decisions when the time is right?

This passage of the two thieves reminds us of our folly. It testifies to the reality that a change of heart may never come. We will rejoice in heaven over the one sinner who repented (Luke 15:7), but, for now, we must lament over the sinner who is lost. This story of the cross is both a triumph and a tragedy. Within a heartbeat we experience elation and, if not careful, are sadly subdued by the things we cannot change. We are responsible for our repentance, but we cannot repent for someone else. As much as we would like, the unrepentant thief remained defiant to the end.

"Forgiveness is an act of the will, and the will can function regardless of the temperature of the heart."
CORRIE TEN BOOM,
The Hiding Place

Are you reading this, knowing that you are not right with God? Maybe your life lies broken. You have been hurt by and have hurt others. You turned to a career seeking happiness or approval from others. Working longer hours has not equated to the satisfaction you seek. You have lived an agonising life and tried to numb the pain with alcohol or drugs. You have lived the tragic and thought the unthinkable. With increasing years and ever fewer choices, the door of your heart lies closed. Too scared to hope and too frightened to love, you are trapped in a prison without doors. You

> *"The fact is that when we forgive someone we not only release them from the burden of our anger and its possible consequences; we release ourselves from the burden of whatever it was they had done to us, and from the crippled emotional state in which we shall go on living if we don't forgive them and instead cling to our anger and bitterness."*
> N.T. WRIGHT,
> *Evil and the Justice of God*

cannot reach out and no one can reach in. Better to live in isolation than to face another rejection.

Convinced that no one has room for you in their hearts, you project your despair heavenwards. Why should God love you when no one on else does? Why should God care? Your life is ebbing away and why should God be interested in the fragments that are left? Pause and join the repentant thief on the cross. Refuse to glance at his colleague in crime. His final few breaths are wasted in empty rhetoric. His venomous words drift upwards but not heavenwards.

Instead, this repentant thief offers hope to us all. It was the fragment of a life but a miracle as great as the feeding of the five thousand. For out of very little, God made an abundant provision. Out of what was left, God gave him paradise.

The cross is a story of relentless love. A picture painted large with the brushstrokes of grace. Against the backdrop of cruelty and injustice, hope rises as a defiant flare. "Today you will be with me in paradise." Oh, what grace, what love, what power to forgive, what goodness of heart! Jesus embraced a dying man and is willing to embrace each of us too. He gave reassurance to a broken man. This man dared to ask Jesus to remember him, and to his relief Jesus said "Yes!" Can you imagine the joy that Jesus's salvation brought to that criminal's heart? Forever let it bring hope and joy to yours.

If you are using this as a four-part Bible study, please refer to Session Four on pages 61–68

Life Blog

It was a bright sunny day proving summer had truly arrived. I was seventeen years old and standing with friends outside the shops. I was on holiday, and life could not have been better.

The oldest in the group wanted a cigarette. He fumbled in his pocket and brought out an empty packet. To his disappointment, no one else had any either. With a sigh and a face of silent resignation, he shoved both hands into his pockets.

I didn't smoke, but I felt his disappointment. He was addicted to nicotine. It was one of the few, if expensive, pleasures he looked forward to. With a cool demeanor and a sharp sense of humour, he was well liked and the type of friend you would go out of your way to help. So being a person of enterprise, I decided to rectify the situation.

I excused myself and went back into the shopping precinct. I knew the layout of the store well (this was before the days of CCTV cameras). I stepped up to the counter and spoke to the girl standing at the till. I pointed to a rather inexpensive item behind her, and she turned around to retrieve the item. In a split second I slid my hand to the other side of the counter where the cigarettes were kept. In one swift motion, I dislodged the packet and placed it into in my Wrangler jacket pocket. After paying for the item she retrieved, I smiled at her and left.

I returned to the group, pulled the packet of cigarettes from my pocket, and won my friend's approval. Everybody was happy. The one who needed it the most lit up, gave a long and satisfying draw on the cigarette, and exhaled with a sigh of relief. Leaving the smoke to linger, we moved on as we made our way into the seaside resort before nightfall.

If only my conscience had remained at the shops. But it followed me with every step I took. This type of conscience was new to me. With every footstep, the realisation of the cause of my angst sank in. It had only been a matter of weeks, but in desperation I had reached out to God and invited him into my life.

Now, the sharp pain of conviction regarding my theft was beginning to disable my youthful steps towards the amusement park. I stopped in my tracks and excused myself from the crowd, who were oblivious to my pang of conscience. They did not know I had stolen the item. The shopkeeper did not even know the item was missing. No amount of rationalisation on my part diluted my disappointment in myself. I knew I had stolen. And more disconcerting, the God I had invited into my life knew I had stolen.

I wrestled in thought for a few moments and returned to the shop. Sheepishly I entered and stood at the back, waiting for customers to pay for their items. With the shop now empty, I approached the sales assistant. I blurted out that I had stolen the cigarettes earlier and that my newfound faith had prompted me to return and pay for the pack. She looked puzzled and then pleased that I had the courage to return. I made recompense for what I had taken. She assured me the shop would not take any further action and thanked me for my honesty — if not my theft.

It was difficult not to feel both pleasure and guilt throughout the day. I regretted my actions in stealing the item. But I was also pleased that I had felt shame and the necessity of confession and restitution. God had taught this imperfect disciple a very valuable lesson.

That day I learned something of the forgiveness of God. The thief on the cross and I had something in common. We recognised our unworthiness and possessed a hope that God was willing to forgive. That is the glory of the cross. That forgiveness extends to the poor in spirit and those who are needy and repentant. Paradise is a gracious gift, not earned, but extended to all those who are willing to say, "Jesus, remember me when you come into your kingdom" (Luke 23:42).

Life Application

1. When the thief spoke of being justly punished, he was acknowledging those things he had done that were wrong. He was aware of his guilt, and often so are we.

With a pen and notepad, draw five columns. At the top of each column, write the following headings: My Sinful Actions, Associated Feelings, Parallel Biblical Characters, God's Response, My Response. Make a list under the heading Sinful Actions of sins that may have troubled you and perhaps still do. Under Associated Feelings, write out or draw how you feel as you reflect upon those sins. What emotion(s) does this situation engender? In the next column, reflect on the biblical characters who may have been engaged in similar activities. From those passages, list God's response to those characters' actions. Reflect upon possible reasons why God either forgave them or continued to judge them because of those actions. In the last column, list your response to what you have discovered. Can you think of any practical way you can make restitution for what you have done? Or take time to ponder how you can apply God's forgiveness to your life.

Use the table on page 38 to help you navigate through this process.

My Sinful Actions	Associated Feelings	Parallel Biblical Characters	God's Response	My Response
I harbored envy and resentment against Ted, a member of my small group in church.	Justification, anger, guilt.	Saul—He envied David and they had worked closely together.	He judged Saul for treating David in that way. God was upset with Saul because he had refused to listen to him.	I want to be careful that I do not let envy, bitterness, or resentment take root in my life. I will make sure that I must refuse to expect Ted to change but ask that God change me. The practical things I will do to avoid resentment: 1. Pray for blessing in Ted's life. 2. Act kindly toward him even when I don't feel it. 3. Ask to find out more about Ted so that I can understand what motivates him, pleases him, or disappoints him.

When you list an action by a particular biblical character, where the forgiveness of God is clearly demonstrated, take a moment to ponder God's grace, and rejoice that God will demonstrate that same grace towards you. As amazing as it may seem, Jesus wanted not only to spend time with the thief in paradise but also in his last few moments with him on earth. He wants to spend time with you right now and share his love and grace with you.

2. With scissors, cut away the column labeled My Sinful Actions. What can you do with that column? You might crumple it up and throw it into the bin. That certainly would take the list out of sight, but it still remains somewhere else in the house. Out of sight is not necessarily out of mind. You may scribble through the items on the list, but marks on the page are a visible reminder to their presence. Instead, consider finding a safe place to destroy the column altogether. Set fire to the piece of paper and place it on a dish until it is completely disintegrated, and then dispose of the ash. At the end of this process, read those liberating words in Colossians 2:13–14 and reflect on "having taken them away." This is what God has done with your sins if you have truly repented from them.

3. Draft a prayer to God. Write briefly, honestly, and in a spirit of gratitude. Acknowledge the particular sin or sins God has forgiven. Thank him for those verses that reminded you of forgiveness, outlining what you love most about God's grace and how his forgiveness has made you feel. If you can take some practical action to show your appreciation for this forgiveness, include it in your prayer, and endeavor to fulfill it as a way of demonstrating your gratitude.

4. At the end of his encounter with Jesus, the repentant thief was promised that he would be in paradise with Jesus that very day. What appeared to be an unfolding tragedy was, in fact, the unveiling of our future hope. A home in heaven is a paradise beyond description. Each one of us may have a favourite place and for many different reasons. A photograph of a holiday destination might conjure memories of family and friends. Possibly the sunset or lake nurtures a feeling of peace and tranquility. Find an image of that place and attach it to this page. For a few moments, reflect on the beauty of this place and thank God for all the reasons why this image is more special than any other. Read aloud the words of 1 Corinthians 2:9.

Points to Ponder
Session One

1. As you read the Introduction, how does is make you feel? Does the description fill you with fear, apprehension, or hope? How would you have sought to provide Sally with support, and what are the most important things to do during such occasions? How would you encourage your local church fellowship to support Sally during such a difficult time? How could these verses be applied to what you have been discussing? (James 1:12; Proverbs 18:2, 13; Ecclesiastes 3:7,4:9-12; Hebrews 13:16; Romans 12:13)

2. When death finally casts its shadow, what do you believe hurts the most? How do you imagine Adam and Eve lived prior to the fall? If we were created to live forever, why is death so difficult? If you have experienced grief, explain to others what has been your greatest comfort.

3. Alistair wrote, "The gospel artist draws this scene in charcoal grey because no palette of colours can be found. Yet we are invited to linger at the cross and look beyond the pain of our grief, to see in the portrait one man of colour set against the backdrop of greys." What words or phrases did you pay particular attention to and why? Read Luke 23:26–49. After considering the entire scene, why is Jesus perhaps painted in colour as you compare him with the crowd? When it comes to sad times like these, how would you describe yourself: painted in colour or grey? Explain your answer.

4. As you read Psalm 22 together, what portions of the psalm are painted in grey and what sections bring colour and hope? Explain how they bring you hope and can be applied to a current situation you are facing.

Points to Ponder

Session Two

1. As Janice's pastor, I can testify to the tremendous resilience she showed during her heartache. How have people and places given you strength during a time of crisis? What Bible verses in particular have you turned to?

2. Have there been times you have spoken, when perhaps it would have been better to remain quiet? If so, share with the group that experience. Why did you feel you had to speak? Upon reflection, what did you learn from that experience?

3. What lessons can we learn from Job 16? As to the mistakes that can be made when dealing with complex situations, what should be avoided, and how we should conduct ourselves? What principles can we apply to our dealings with others?

4. What are the key elements that the repentant thief acknowledged in his declaration (Luke 23:40–42)? What hope can be found in Jesus's response to the repentant thief (Luke 23:43)? Why may some people object to a thief being forgiven, when morally upright people may not be? How may these biblical passages help us in dealing with such objections, and what hope do they present to everyone? (Isaiah 64:6; James 4:17; Romans 3:23–24; 1 John 1:9)

5. When you read John 14:1–6, what do you look forward to most about what Jesus declares?

Points to Ponder
Session Three

1. Alistair wrote, "How would our priorities change if we knew we had very few hours to live? We may prioritise our lives, sharpen our reflections, and choose our words more carefully. The recognition of our own mortality focuses our thoughts. We reflect upon the direction of our lives, the relationships we have nurtured—perhaps even those we need to amend." What priorities would you seek to change? What would you celebrate the most as you reflected back over your life?

2. Read Matthew 5:24 in your group, and as you reflect on its teaching, what are the challenges it presents? Also read the quote from N.T Wright on page 30. What problems can emerge from not being reconciled with people, and how may that effect your relationship with God? Alistair implied that there may be certain things we may need to amend. If so, allow the group to spend a moment in quiet reflection.

3. Reflect on N.T Wright's quote on page 20. What do you believe he is attempting to say? How do you feel about what he says? How may Jesus's response to both thieves demonstrate his point?

4. Relentless grace is a beautiful truth of Scripture. As you compare these two passages Isaiah 61:1–2 and Luke 4:18–19, what is missing from the Isaiah passage, and why has Jesus deliberately chosen to omit it? If you were attempting to identify particular individuals or groups of people described in Luke 4:18–19, who are the poor, the prisoner, blind, and the oppressed within your community? And how does God's message of hope apply to them? How could the church make that hope a reality? Reflect on Bruggemann's quote on page 25. How does this statement bring both a challenge and hope?

Points to Ponder

Session Four

1. Jesus was endlessly mocked while he was on the cross. People called out to him, "If you are God, save yourself!" Jesus could have saved himself, but he did not. What are your reflections on Jesus's sacrificial love? What do his choices teach about the nature of sacrifice? What does that teach about love?

2. Jesus maintained compassion for others while facing his own death, even pronouncing forgiveness for the sinners who mocked his crucifixion and the thief who hung at his side. How can Christians extend Christ-like grace to a hurting world?

3. Why do you think Jesus forgave the criminal who took responsibility for his crimes, acknowledged that Jesus was God, and asked to be remembered when Jesus went into his kingdom? What do each criminal's words reveal about the state of their hearts? What kept the unrepentant thief from accepting Christ?

4. When is it too late to accept Jesus into your life? What reasons do people give for waiting to accept Jesus as their Saviour?

5. There are many examples of people's lives changing after one encounter with the Lord: the woman at the well, the lepers whom Jesus healed. How do our lives change when we encounter Christ? Can you describe the moment Christ changed your life?

6. Which hymns or praise songs celebrate God's forgiveness? Which images or phrases in these songs inspire your heart to receive the grace that God offers to you?

7. Jesus promised the repentant thief, "Today you will be with me in paradise." What comfort might this have given the repentant thief? It is understandable that we have a fear of dying, but how does the statement "Today, you will be with me in paradise" help reduce those fears? What comfort can we derive from Bible passages such as Psalm 9:9; 116:12; Lamentations 3:31–33; John 14:16–17?

References

Brueggemann, Walter. *The Collected Sermons of Walter Bruggemann.* Louisville, KY: Westminster John Knox Press, 2011.

Lucado, Max. *Grace: More Than We Deserve, Greater Than We Imagine.* Nashville, TN: Thomas Nelson, 2014.

Navone, John. *Seeking God in Story.* Collegeville, MN: The Liturgical Press, 1990.

Neumark, Heidi. *Breathing Space.* Boston, MA: Beacon Press, 2003.

Ten Boom, Corrie. *The Hiding Place.* Grand Rapids, MI: Chosen Books, 1971.

Wright, N. T. *Evil and the Justice of God.* Westmont, IL: IVP Press, 2011.

Other Books Written by the Author

Halloween

Happy Holiday or Dangerous Deception?

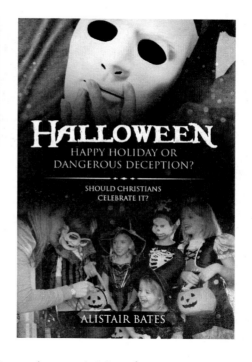

Excerpt:

I WAS NEW to the congregation, and I am not a killjoy. I was hoping to avoid sharing my strong convictions on the subject until I had earned the congregation's trust and respect. Planning to arrange alternative activities for our young daughter, we presumed her attendance would not be missed. We were not afforded that luxury, however. At the Sunday morning service before the festival, a church member asked our four-year-old daughter if she would be attending. She innocently replied, "Oh, no! My mummy and daddy won't allow me to go to Halloween parties." It was neither the time nor place to enter into a discussion, especially given the slightly embarrassing revelation. To the congregation's credit, without any discussion the following year's celebration was dropped from the church calendar.

Already you might be thinking I have some extreme views toward Halloween and want to eliminate anything "fun" related to this holiday that might bring children (or their parents) enjoyment. I understand your concerns! The context of my disquiet can be traced back to 2001, when I was the pastor of a church in Northern Ireland, a congregation that God had abundantly blessed. In 2000, our average attendance was eighty-seven; however, during the first year-and-a-half of my ministry there, the congregation had grown to approximately 130 in weekly attendance. During that time many people had become Christians. Even the age profile of our church had changed. In 2000, we had a few young children. By the end of 2001, 33 percent of our congregation was below the age of fourteen. These were truly exciting times, until a visitor arrived.

At first this visitor was unobtrusive and drew little attention to herself. She participated in services and became increasingly involved in church life. But strangely, her presence began to affect people negatively. During this period, inexplicable events started to happen...

Other Books Written by the Author

Vital Signs

Book 2

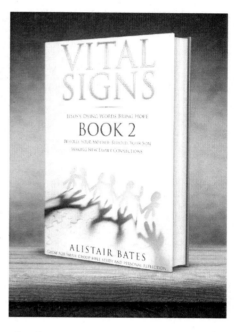

Excerpt:

EVERY MOTHER has aspirations for her children. What did Mary imagine when she held her infant son?

What might your mother have imagined as she held you for the first time?

How can a young woman wrap her mind around the profound gift she brought into the world?

Lying in her arms was the Hope of the world, a Promise of new life, new beginnings. Would the cross cast a shadow over this hope, or in his dying breath cast light on new relationships and responsibilities?

When Mary and Joseph took Jesus to the temple, Simeon said, "And a sword will pierce your own soul too." (Luke 2:35) This beautiful, perfect baby would bring her great joy but also be the source of heartbreaking pain. She would be privileged to see his first steps, hear his first words, and watch his first miracle. That first demonstration of his uniqueness had been at her request. Yet the miracle of changing water into wine became the opportunity for Jesus to establish some distance between himself and his mother.

Though her earthly son, he had a heavenly Father. He was not just a son, he was the Saviour of the world. While never a crowd pleaser, Jesus had pleased the crowds many times. He had been attentive to people who were hurting, lonely, and broken. With gentle commands, he had rebuilt broken lives. The lame had taken their first steps, and the blind watched their first sunset. The leper could embrace their family and the lost could find their way home.

Yet in dismay Jesus's mother had watched the adulation of crowds turn to scorn. She witnessed family members misinterpret his actions and religious leaders conspire against him. The chants of the crowd "crucify him," would haunt her, and Peter's denial left her feeling betrayed. As the garments lay scattered on the dusty ground, she would think of soldiers who had cast lots for his clothes just moments before. Those very same soldiers' callous hearts had not only cradled the dice but driven a crown of thorns unto his head. It was not just the cries of his accusers that pierced her heart that day but their actions too. In the recesses of her heart, Jesus's mother knew he would face no natural death. But it seemed that he did not want to avert it. She maintained the grace she showed when the angel of the Lord came to her, and she replied "Let it be done unto me according to your word" (Luke 1:38 NIV). She was in the company of her son's best friends at the foot of the cross.

Just as Simeon prophesied, on that Good Friday when Jesus's mother stood at the cross that wore her dying son, a sword pierced her heart. Even as an obedient disciple, she could not avoid her heart being wracked by pain. Was this the price she had to pay for bearing a son who had to die such a death? She had much to ponder. How much she knew of the plan that would unfold is difficult to know. Certainly though, Mary may have been confused and perplexed if she had hoped that part of Jesus's plan was to liberate his people from Roman oppression. If so, how disappointed she must have felt! Or was she outraged, weeping with anger and sadness at the extreme injustice of it all? Not only was an innocent man suffering the scandal of lies and deceit, the man was her son. She stood there, watching her earthly son mistreated by many and rejected by the majority. As darkness descended on the hill, it also cascaded into her heart.

Don't miss out on Book 2
as it will soon be available in printed format.